Observing
the Rests

52 Personal Devotions for the Choir Member

Terry W. York

Abingdon Press
Nashville

OBSERVING THE RESTS
52 Personal Devotions for the Choir Member

Copyright © 2003 by Abingdon Press

All rights reserved.

This book is printed on acid-free, recycled paper.

ISBN 0-687-04748-X

03 04 05 06 07 08 09 10 11 12 — 10 9 8 7 6 5 4 3 2 1

MANUFACTURED IN THE UNITED STATES OF AMERICA

I leave work's daily rule
And come here to this restful place
Where music stirs the pool
And from high stations of the air
Fall notes of wordless grace,
Strewn remnants of the primal
*Sabbath's hymn. **

Wendell Berry

* From *A Timbered Choir* by Wendell Berry. Copyright © 1998 by Wendell Berry.
Reprinted by permission of Counterpoint Press, a member of Perseus Books, L. L. C.

Preface

Sound is enriched by silence. Music's sound would soon grow monotonous if it were not for music's silence. In music, the rest is as important as the note. Orchestrated silence allows for the processing of what has just taken place. It is a moment to prepare for whatever may come next.

Rests come in a variety of durations because of the intensity of silence in any given instance. Sometimes a little silence is all we should take. Sometimes we are lost in glorious silence in which time stands still. In life, in music, there must be periods of rest.

Sabbath. Centering. These important disciplines take place in silence. The still small voice that will not shout can only be heard in silence. God's silence is far more profound than our words and music.

"We need both for our full development; the joy of the sense of sound; and the equally great joy of its absence."** We are in choir because singing is a joy. Silence is a joy as well. It is rare as gold and often as refreshing as a cool drink on a hot day. But, there are times when we fear silence. We must not use the making of music as a means of suppressing the still small voice that echoes in the depths of our heart. Rather than masking suppressed pain, music can be used to heal, restoring the beauty of silence. We do, indeed, need both the sense of sound and the solitude of silence for our full development.

Sing from the depths of your silence. Be silent in the depths to which music will take you.

Observing the rests is more than a musical discipline. It is a life discipline. Observing the rests is musical formation and spiritual formation.

Terry W. York
School of Music and
George W. Truett Theological Seminary
Baylor University, Waco, Texas

** Madeleine L'Engle, *A Circle of Quiet* (San Francisco: Harper, 1972), p. 134.

Fall
Week 1

Scripture: "*So then, a sabbath rest still remains for the people of God; for those who enter God's rest also cease from their labors as God did from his. Let us therefore make every effort to enter that rest, so that no one may fall through such disobedience as theirs.*" *(Heb. 4:9-11)*

Sometimes rest is difficult. You know about the little eighth rests that appear in a fast and busy rhythmic pattern. They are difficult to observe. But when you fail to observe them, you throw everyone around you off. When rests are prescribed or assigned to your part, there's a reason—and it is not because there were no notes that would fit that space. The rests are important in the overall scheme of things. Often, missing a rest is more disruptive than missing a note.

The Composer has written some rests into our lives. These are often referred to as Sabbath. One day a week is to be observed as Sabbath. We sleep a certain number of hours each day. We are encouraged to "Be still, and know that I am God!" (Ps. 46:10). Occasionally, people take sabbatical leaves, time to get away from the classroom, office, or pulpit to refresh body, mind, and soul. To miss these rests is to risk making sounds when you're not supposed to, throwing the rhythm of the work out of whack. Everyone around you will be affected.

God chooses to do much of God's work through us, but God is not dependent upon us in the same way that we are dependent upon God. That tongue twister is meant to make the point that those who believe that God is able to handle things should enter into God's rest—God's ability and capacity to rest. When God calls us to rest, we will only keep on working if we think God doesn't understand the situation. We cannot believe that God is all-knowing and in control and then think it's a mistake when God calls us to cease from our labors. God rested. Are we more aware, committed, and necessary than God?

Observe the rests, no matter how difficult. If you don't, you'll mess up the music.

Prayer: Give us the faith in you to rest. Help us to remember the Sabbath and thus, keep it holy. In Jesus' name. Amen.

Fall
Week 2

Hymn: "*All Praise to Thee, My God, This Night,*" *stanza 1: "All praise to thee, my God, this night, for all the blessings of the light! Keep me, O keep me, King of kings, beneath thine own almighty wings." (Words by Thomas Ken, 1674)*

We rehearse it every night, and don't even think about it. We rehearse putting ourselves totally in God's care. No matter how many locks are on our doors, how many burglar alarms and smoke detectors are in place, when we go to sleep at night, we rest most deeply and fully in the arms of Jesus. Our faith is the last blanket that we pull up under our chin.

We remember Jesus lamenting "Jerusalem, Jerusalem, . . . How often have I desired to gather your children together as a hen gathers her brood under her wings, and you were not willing!" (Matt. 23:37). We answer back just before we go to sleep, "Keep me, O keep me, King of kings, beneath thine own almighty wings." Those may not be our exact words, but they express the prayer that closes our eyes.

Then dawns the day and we take over. Jesus pulled the night shift. If we are not careful we will regard the daytime Jesus the same way we regard the daytime locks, alarms, and detectors; in place, but not as critical to our well-being. "The blessings of the light" include the awareness that Jesus offers his wings in the day, just as he did during the night. Now in his glorified body, he never sleeps. Little brood, his daycare is fully dependable.

Having run the race full circle under a wing and a prayer, we make our way back to the pillow. Observing the rest just before we give ourselves to it, we reach for the lamp and the prayer. "All praise to you, my God, this night, for all the blessings of the light!" (click). "Keep me, O keep me, King of kings, beneath thine own almighty wings."

Prayer: Dear God, we thank you that you are with us always. Help us to always be aware of your presence. Help us to always be thankful. In Jesus' name. Amen.

Hymn: "*Great Is Thy Faithfulness,*" refrain: "*Great is thy faithfulness! Morning by morning new mercies I see; all I have needed thy hand hath provided; great is thy faithfulness, Lord, unto me!*" (*Words by Thomas O. Chisholm, 1923*)

What do we see when we wake up from our rest? We see that God has been faithful. Even when we wake up to the realization that the tragedy we experienced actually did happen, we are strengthened deep in our soul, for as the psalmist has reminded us, "still the Lord made the sunrise." When we wake up to the realization that the project or challenge is still there, we have the hope of the new day and the strength of the night's rest. God is faithful. When we wake up to the fact that we have hurt someone and forgiveness needs to be asked, God gives the mercy of a chance to go see the person and say what needs to be said. Morning by morning new mercies I see.

We are not the first to wake up to the fact of God's faithfulness and mercy; it has happened since the beginning of time. Peter experienced the mercies of the new day when the resurrected Christ fixed breakfast for him on the seashore of Galilee. Morning by morning, awakening by awakening, dawn after dawn, new mercies we see.

Sunday, many in the congregation will be resting on their laurels. They will be tired from long periods of shallow rest. They have forgotten that morning mercies exist. They wake up to a frustrating to-do list that makes more noise in their soul than the alarm makes in their ear. They go to work knowing that all the pressure will "still be there." They get to work while it is still dark—the light of God's faithfulness and mercy has not dawned on them.

Sing them awake. Open their hearts, minds, and ears. Lead them to learn and sing, "Morning by morning new mercies I see." Help them to know that at the end of the day and at the end of the month all they will have needed, God's hand will have provided. Sing the sun up above their low horizon.

Prayer: Dear God, fill our songs with your sunrise. Fill our songs with your hope and the assurance of your presence. Sing through us every morning. In Jesus' name. Amen.

Fall
Week 4

Scripture: "*And the four living creatures, each of them with six wings, are full of eyes all around and inside. Day and night without ceasing they sing, 'Holy, holy, holy, the Lord God the Almighty, who was and is and is to come.'*" *(Rev. 4:8)*

We only have two eyes and they must close from time to time. We cannot sing day and night without ceasing. It is good that the heavenly beings are able to worship God ceaselessly, because God is worthy of it. We know their song, or at least several variations on the theme, and we join them in singing, "Holy, holy, holy." But we have another song to sing and it should fill our limited waking hours. It is the song of redemption.

Only two eyes, no wings, and regularly in need of sleep, we have more to sing about than the angels, cherubim, seraphim, and all the other hosts of heaven. Deep sleep is, in a sense, praise to God, because we aren't staying awake taking care of God's business. We praise God by exercising faith in God. But while we are awake, full of eyes watching, watching out, watching over, analyzing, processing, we can fail to worship, fail to sing a wide-awake "Holy, holy, holy."

One of the ways we can sing without ceasing is to take our hymns and anthems with us. Not in our folders, but in our hearts. Lines from our songs can surface while walking down the hall or sitting at a stoplight. "Holy, holy, holy," or one of its derivatives, can be on our lips or minds frequently, if not "without ceasing." These songs are one of the benefits of singing in the choir. Memorize them, internalize them, so that your waking moments can be given to worship.

Again, we have a responsibility to the congregation. They don't attend choir rehearsal. They don't go over the songs time and time again. Therefore, it becomes our responsibility to sing memorably on Sunday mornings. This takes time: time in rehearsal, time on our own, and time on Sunday mornings, but it is time well spent, for we sing "Holy, holy, holy," to the One "who was and is and is to come."

Prayer: Dear God, help us to be constantly aware of your presence and your love for us. Help us to worship you in all that we do. In Jesus' name. Amen.

Hymn: *"The Church's One Foundation," stanza 4: "Mid toil and tribulation, and tumult of her war, she waits the consummation of peace forevermore; till, with the vision glorious, her longing eyes are blest, and the great church victorious shall be the church at rest." (Words by Samuel J. Stone, 1866)*

We are singing the church through its battles. The church battles with the world and, unfortunately, with itself. The church is at war with the world because the values of the kingdom of this world and the kingdom of heaven are opposites; they are at odds with each other. We are to be in the world, but not of it, and that puts us in a somewhat hostile position.

The church also battles within itself over music preferences, worship styles, theology, and doctrine. The first set of battles is to be expected, this world is not a friend to grace. The second set, to the extent that it causes warfare, is to be lamented. All the while, on both fronts, the church is singing, led by its choirs. We sing "the church's one foundation is Jesus Christ her Lord" to strengthen our resolve to worship God and no other gods. We sing "the church's one foundation is Jesus Christ her Lord" to remind the church's many traditions of our common foundation and calling. Like the Levites of the Old Testament, our choirs and their music have important responsibilities and roles.

Mid toil, tribulation, and tumult we sing. We sing of peace and the glorious vision of heaven and the church's ultimate victory in Christ. Frightened, tired, frustrated, unsure at times, we stand each Sunday, nevertheless, and sing. We sing toward the day when "the great church victorious shall be the church at rest." What a day, what a song, what a mission!

Prayer: Dear God, help us to sing with the understanding of our place in the church's journey through this world. Strengthen us for the task. In Jesus' name. Amen.

Fall
Week 6

Scripture: "But in the seventh year there shall be a sabbath of complete rest for the land." (Lev. 25:4a)

Though I have a deep reverence for "the land," I know nothing about farming. I'm aware, from high school classes, about crop rotation for the purpose of chemical balance in the soil. But that's it. Even so, I've wondered from time to time that if crop rotation is good, would an occasional rest from growing anything at all be better? Then I read the Leviticus passage above. Rest for the land. What an interesting thought.

I'm not a farmer, but I love the farmland that surrounds the little town in Missouri where my parents live. The land seems at peace. That is, it doesn't seem to be under the stress that is imposed on the land that "moved to town." There it seems fields must be rescued from uselessness by being paved into parking lots. Land must hold big buildings and shopping centers that treat it like a doormat. An innocent pasture or marsh becomes an international airport, a lily pad for big silver frogs.

Then it dawns on me. I'm transposing my feelings onto the land. It's me who needs the rest. It's me who needs a sea of grass bowing in the wind. It's me who needs the change of pace from rows of cars to rows of corn. It's me who needs to do nothing for a while except feel the breeze on my face and smell newly mown hay.

Or is it just me? Maybe it is, in fact, me *and* the land that need a vacation, quiet, and a slow natural pace. Maybe we're closer to the land than we think. Maybe telling us to give the land a rest is just another way that God tells us to rest now and then.

Choirs, choir members, rest now and then. Give your songs time to return to the soil. Listen to the breeze of the melodies and rhythms that are still sounding in your soul. Think on the texts of your hymns and anthems. Remember them at their pace. Let them grow within you with no other purpose than to bring you rest.

Prayer: Dear God, slow us down, grow us deep, and let us feel the breeze of your spirit, unencumbered by things we have constructed. In Jesus' name. Amen.

Hymn: "Near to the Heart of God," stanza 1: "There is a place of quiet rest, near to the heart of God; a place where sin cannot molest, near to the heart of God." (Words by Cleland B. McAfee, 1903)

It's amazing how much energy it takes to deal with noise. Noise must be dealt with. It cannot be ignored without working at it. Noise demands attention. That's why I won't eat in noisy restaurants. The noise won't leave me alone. Perhaps that's why noisy people *are* noisy—they need attention. Perhaps that's why commercials are always louder than the TV show they interrupt. Noise demands attention.

Silence invites you in. No wonder Cleland McAfee depicts nearness to God as a place of quiet rest. The Holy Spirit does not shout or demand. The Holy Spirit invites. Jesus said, "Come unto me," not "Get over here." I always wonder about noisy worship. Is God noisy? Was Jesus noisy? Is the Holy Spirit noisy?

What is the place of noisy worship? "Make a joyful noise to the LORD, all the earth" (Ps. 98:4). There's our permission, indeed, our instruction. "But the LORD is in his holy temple; let all the earth keep silence before him!" (Hab. 2:20). We may not read Habakkuk as often as the Psalms, but that does not diminish Habakkuk's place in Holy Scripture.

Perhaps worship and rest are different enough that we are comparing apples and oranges here. Worship is a gift we give. Rest is a gift we receive. We may be more skilled in worship and thus more prone to being boisterous in the doing of it. Rest, on the other hand, is something we know much less about. Often, the only time we engage in it, we're asleep. We are going to be quieter concerning the things we don't know much about. We have come to define worship as something at which we can be successful. It's hard to measure the success of rest. Doing is often more noisy than being.

Actually, I think it's the apples and oranges thing. Receiving a gift is something you should do quietly, with humble gratitude. Worship is something God initiates. We couldn't do it if God didn't initiate it and energize it. But it is a gift we give back to God. We may be noisy in the giving of it, but I think God receives the gift of worship quietly.

The hymn writer knew what he was talking about. There *is* a place of quiet rest, near to the heart of God.

Prayer: Dear God, thank you for the privilege of worshiping you. Thank you also for providing for us a place of quiet rest. Help us to give ourselves to you in both ways. In Jesus' name. Amen.

Hymn: *"How Firm a Foundation," stanza 5: "The soul that on Jesus still leans for repose, I will not, I will not desert to its foes; that soul, though all hell should endeavor to shake, I'll never, no, never, no, never forsake."* (*Words by "K" in* Rippon's Selection of Hymns, *1787*)

I'm reminded of my first experience taking a nap in a hammock. Nothing looked more restful. Tied between two trees, moving slightly in the breeze, it was poetically symbolic of resting in my mother's arms as an infant. I had seen other people sleep in the hammock. Their snoring was like a deep song of peace. I would take my turn in the suspended cradle. Plop!

I was trying to get in the hammock the same way I always got into my sturdy bed. There were no legs. My rest was stretched out between two trees. I did not know how to give myself to the arms that would hold me. After a few more quick trips to the ground, I learned to lean. I can't describe the technique. "Leaning" and letting the hammock do the work, is as close as I can come to a helpful description. I can tell you that it was like floating on air, almost a spiritual thing. I stayed awake for a while, not sure how much of my success could be attributed to the hammock and how much was due to my careful balance. Sometime into my calculations, I fell asleep. Deep rest, the poetry of "repose" seems a more fitting word.

When I awoke, I realized I had let down my guard, slept, and survived. The hammock had not forsaken or discharged me. I was still in it, now rested *and* confident. I came back to the hammock from time to time. Sometimes for rest, other times to make sure I could still get in it, practicing so I wouldn't fall if others were watching. Listen to the hymn stanza again: "The soul that on Jesus still leans for repose, I will not, I will not desert to its foes; that soul, though all hell should endeavor to shake, I'll never, no, never, no, never forsake."

I love the last line of this hymn, "I'll never, no, never, no, never forsake." It reminds me of Peter getting to say three times (once for each denial): "You know I love you." Lean on Christ's foundation of love today.

Prayer: Dear God, thank you for holding us in your everlasting arms. Thank you for the firm foundation that feels like floating. In Jesus' name. Amen.

Fall
Week 9

Hymn: " 'Tis So Sweet to Trust in Jesus," stanza 1: " 'Tis so sweet to trust in Jesus, and to take him at his word; just to rest upon his promise, and to know, 'Thus saith the Lord.'" (Words by Louisa M. R. Stead, 1882)

Sometimes it's a wonderful feeling to know that you are not in charge. As much as we like to be recognized as leaders in our particular field of interest, now and then it is good to know that we are not in charge. As much as we may think we know more about music than our choir director, it's good to know that the rehearsal and the performance are ultimately his or her responsibilities. The outcome is in someone else's hands. That alone can cause you to breathe deeply and rest. We could rest much more often and much more deeply than we do if we would apply that to our spiritual lives as well.

There are promises throughout the Bible that could make life a happier and more abundant journey for us if we would simply "rest upon" them. It's as if God keeps saying, "Here, let me get that for you," and we keep saying, "No, I've got it." But the things God wants to help us with are God-sized burdens. We become weary and worn out if we try to carry them in our own strength.

Maybe we're trying to impress God. Maybe we're trying to help God. When we insist on doing God-sized things, we are certainly doubting God. What are some of the God-sized things we take on ourselves? Maintaining joy, integrity, and direction in the midst of setbacks, disappointments, and temptations; money management and time management; worry about the challenges we will face tomorrow; illnesses beyond the reach of medicine—are you getting tired? Does all this have a rather bitter taste to it? " 'Tis so sweet to trust in Jesus, and to take him at his word; just to rest upon his promise, and to know, 'Thus saith the Lord.' " Remember the words of the psalmist: "O taste and see that the LORD is good; happy are those who take refuge in him" (Ps. 34:8).

Prayer: Dear God, thank you for the promises in your word and the joy, assurance, and rest they bring. Help us to rest in them more often and more deeply. In Jesus' name. Amen.

Scripture: *"But my mind could not rest because I did not find my brother Titus there."* *(2 Cor. 2:13a)*

Paul could not stay in a place of opportunity and rest because his brother Titus wasn't there. Christians who have learned to rest in the Lord will be concerned for their brothers and sisters who have not done so. Such rest is too dear, too important, and too enriching to keep it to oneself. Badgering someone with your formula of rest is not restful for you or them. But to fail to inform a busy or troubled brother or sister about the rest God offers is to withhold love.

The same is true for those in need of physical rest. Christians should be sensitive to this and offer help that will result in rest. When our children were young, my wife and I often had babysitting agreements with friends who also had children. We would baby-sit for each other, without charge, allowing each couple times of rest. There are other ways to lift someone else's burdens from time to time. Paul, the busy evangelist, was concerned that Titus was not in the place of opportunity and rest.

What would it mean to the fellowship and unity of your choir if you looked for ways to help one another carve out times of rest? What would it mean to the choir's ministry if the choir, in addition to singing on Sunday mornings, provided times of rest for young couples with children and for other weary caregivers in the congregation? Do you think the congregation might pay a bit more attention to the message of the anthems? What would it mean in the life and work of the church if nonmusical actions undergirded the message of the music?

The choir's ministry can and should invite others into the opportunity and rest that God offers. We are brothers and sisters in Christ. Perhaps in our resting in the Lord and in our ministry through music we can, like Paul, come to the place where we will say, "But my mind could not rest because I did not find my brother."

Prayer: Dear God, help me to share the rest I find in you with brother and sisters who are weary. In Jesus' name. Amen.

Fall
Week 11

Hymn: "Come, Thou Long-Expected Jesus," stanza 1: "Come, thou long-expected Jesus, born to set thy people free; from our fears and sins release us, let us find our rest in thee." (Words by Charles Wesley, 1744)

For about a year now, we have either given up on rest or we have been seeking it to no avail. Weekends and vacations take forever to come and then fly by. Hobbies and similar projects have been placed lower on the to-do list each time they have tried to make their way to the top. As fulfilling as work at the office or around the house might be, there is little rest there. Even our most satisfying relationships require something of us, and while they are pleasant, they are not always restful. Where shall we turn for the deep rest the soul desires?

Charles Wesley's hymn, "Come, Thou Long-Expected Jesus," gets right to the solution. We are to find our rest in Jesus. We are reminded of this during Advent. God has not forgotten us. Jesus was born to set us free from fears and sin, to be our strength and consolation, to be our hope. The greatest hope may be that we might take this truth from the realm of facts we know to actual, daily practice. We want to make this the joy of our hearts, not just the truth in our minds.

We do, in fact, employ in our daily living much of what we have learned from Jesus' example and teachings. We participate in the salvation he made possible. But to be honest, there is still an unfulfilled expectation. We are still longing for the practical employment of being set free from fears and sins. We are still looking forward to finding the rest in Jesus that becomes a part of who we are and how we "do" life. We want *that* long-expected Jesus to come. We are ready for *that* rest.

The key to that coming and the fulfillment of that promise is found in the second stanza of the hymn: "By thine own eternal spirit rule in all our hearts alone; by thine all-sufficient merit, raise us to thy glorious throne." It is a matter of spirit. We must let the mind of Christ be in us. We must allow the Holy Spirit to guide us in attitude, response, relationships, and decision making. Sing the hymn as a prayer, daily, several times throughout the day.

Prayer: Come, thou long-expected Jesus, by thine own eternal spirit rule in my heart. By thine all-sufficient merit, raise me to thy glorious throne. It is in your name I pray. Amen.

Scripture: "*Six days you shall work, but on the seventh day you shall rest; even in plowing time and in harvest time you shall rest.*" *(Exod. 34:21)*

If we see singing in the choir on Sunday as work, we need to reconsider. We are to rest on the Sabbath. I don't think that means to stop singing and leading in worship. I think it means to see our singing in choir as honoring God's "sign forever between me and the people." The sign is six days of work and one day of rest (Exod. 31:17). God did it. We are to honor God by participating in the sequence and pace established from the beginning. Worship should be rejuvenating, even for those in leadership—perhaps especially for those involved in worship leadership because we get to see God at work through humans firsthand. That's always encouraging.

Sometimes we have responsibilities that seemingly won't wait for us to take our day of rest. Moses saw that coming. If there are deadlines that won't wait, they are the deadlines set by nature and the changing seasons. Even for those of us who are not farmers, the seasons affect our living and being. The end of vacations, the beginning of school, the press of Thanksgiving and holiday plans that barely let us swallow our turkey—these are the urban seasonal changes that won't wait. However, God tells us in our passage for today, "even in plowing time and in harvest time you shall rest." Those times don't wait. The weather and the planting/growing/harvesting times have the inertia of the spinning earth behind them; even so, "you shall rest."

By now you are gearing up for the music of Advent and Christmas. Start early and work diligently so that you can rest "even in" the time of rehearsing and performing. "Six days you shall work [extra or bonus rehearsals], but on the seventh day you shall rest [be rejuvenated by leading in worship on Sunday]; [so that] even in plowing time and in harvest time [the holiday rush] you shall rest."

Enjoy the season.

Prayer: Dear God, let this year be the year in which I rest, even in the back-to-school and holiday rush. In Jesus' name. Amen.

Advent/Christmas
Week 1

Scripture: "So God blessed the seventh day and hallowed it, because on it God rested from all the work that he had done in creation." (Gen. 2:3)

The grand pause in the "Hallelujah" chorus of Handel's *Messiah* is well known to all of us. Some of us feel a closer kinship to it than others because we have sung an enthusiastic, if unscheduled, solo right in the middle of it. We get caught up in the re-creating of beautiful music and the thought of stopping for a moment doesn't occur to us, so we forget. Our "hallelujahs" are rolling and the violins are "sawing," all four voice parts are finally singing at the same time, the little D trumpet finally gets to play, and it's all so successful and organized and impressive, and just before the big finish—rest.

The conductor's fortitude is measured by how long he or she holds this rest, holds the breath of all singers, players, and listeners. For an instant our lives are in the hands of Handel and the conductor. We are being crushed by silence. All that we have sung to this point rushes up against us, pressing us against the far wall of the grand pause. How appropriate that we break the silence by exhaling a group "hallelujah!" We will be singing to a congregation that is probably feeling rushed and pushed as well. Listening to *Messiah,* or whatever you are singing this Advent and Christmas, will be a pause in their rushing. Dedicate yourselves to making it a grand pause. The choir can help the congregation find within themselves a "hallelujah" that they can exhale with calm satisfaction.

Observe the rests for the congregation *and* for yourselves. Observe the big one near the end if you are doing the "Hallelujah" chorus this year. But also observe the smaller ones—quiet times with family and friends, moments in front of the fireplace, silent worship before God. Before long, carolers are going to try to sing a few minutes of rest into your frantic pace. Let them. There may well be wings under their coats.

Prayer: Dear God, help us to hear the *little* bells this season. Help us to see the moments of rest when you send them our way and help us to observe them as little holidays within the holidays. In Jesus' name. Amen.

Hymn: "More Love to Thee, O Christ," stanza 2: "Once earthly joy I craved, sought peace and rest; now thee alone I seek, give what is best. This all my prayer shall be: More love, O Christ, to thee." (Words by Elizabeth P. Prentiss, 1869)

It makes sense. The more love and devotion we give to Jesus, the more we will rest in him. Energy and focus diverted from what this world says is best, to what Jesus says is best, gives the world's emptiness less opportunity to use us or disappoint us. The more we are fully Christ's, the more fully we rest. Devotion to Jesus strengthens us to handle the world better.

Musically, we see this especially clearly as we approach Advent and Christmas. The freshness and warm memories associated with the secular music of Christmas lasts for about two shopping trips. They then become background music for madness. But the carols of the church and in the church focus our love and devotion on the baby of Christmas. That renewal of the true meaning of Christmas helps us to be more Christian in the midst of the secular holiday hassle. The carols of Christmas give what is best. They help us process the carols of consumerism.

Sing the rich carols of Advent's hope and the Gift of Christmas into the ringing ears of the congregation. It is a sorely needed ministry. In this regard, we sing against the gods. We don't try to out shout them. We merely sing the truth against the tinsel. The short moments and quick glances of the real Christmas that we may sing across someone's path in the sanctuary or in the mall will probably be the nicest gift they receive this year. We can trust Jesus to "give what is best."

Our singing is never more important than at this time of year. Sing the simple truth of the birth of Jesus. Let the weary shoppers find rest, rest in giving more love to Christ.

Prayer: Dear God, sing through me the simple, gentle truth of Christmas. In Jesus' name. Amen.

Advent/Christmas
Week 3

Hymn: "What Child Is This," stanza 1: "What child is this who, laid to rest, on Mary's lap is sleeping? Whom angels greet with anthems sweet, while shepherds watch are keeping?" (Words by William C. Dix, 1865)

What child, indeed. What was God thinking? God the Son entered the human race at its weakest point. The whole plan was as fragile as the ancient infant mortality rate. The caretakers were young people in transit. They were a stable away from being out on the street. We wouldn't think of taking a newborn to a petting zoo, yet Jesus' crib was a farm animal's feed trough. What child is this?

Actually, choir members should take great encouragement from the circumstances of the birth of Christ. Our weak voices are in keeping with how the gospel was born. We have a chance at being effective. Even now, the gospel is born at humanity's weakest point: confession of our inabilities.

"This," the story and the carol answer, "this is Christ the King, whom shepherds guard and angels sing; haste, haste to bring him laud, the babe, the son of Mary." Well, what do you know? The Savior out here in the barn? Did God miss the targeted hotel? No. God was and always is, right on target: the humble, the life-made or self-made humble heart. See this stable? See this couple? See this pattern? What child is this? He is the child of God's plan.

We must receive the music in our folders humbly. Practice as if we were the new messengers of the angels' song and present the music as if we were asking royalty to come to the barn. Our music asks the question. Let our music also sing the answer. "This is Christ the King."

Prayer: Dear God, help us to handle the gospel as if we had a baby on our lap, humbly, carefully. Sing through us the good news that the baby comes to turn our weakness into strength. In Jesus' name. Amen.

Hymn: "Lo, How a Rose E'er Blooming," stanza 2: "Isaiah 'twas foretold it, the Rose I have in mind; with Mary we behold it, the Virgin Mother kind. To show God's love aright, she bore to us a Savior, when half spent was the night." (Words: 15th century German; translation by Theodore Baker, 1894)

The night is supposed to be the portion of our daily twenty-four hours during which we sleep; this is our deepest rest. For many, the time to fall asleep becomes the time when their deepest concerns and fears crop up like weeds trampled down during the day. They are afraid to go to sleep. It is as if the night waits in ambush for them.

Jesus was born in and into the middle of the night; Bethlehem's night and humankind's night. As small, unnoticed, and out-of-the-way as a sprout among the weeds, the Savior entered the darkness. Mary's cries of pain were muffled by the surrounding cries of the world. The water and blood of birth flowed; blood as if thorns or nails had torn flesh. A Rose was blooming and night could now be a time of true rest.

Shepherds would see light in the night. Eventually wise men would see light in the night. Oh, that the sleepless could see the little night-light; the light of the one who forgives, who protects the soul, who brings peace. The Rose can make its way up and out through pain and bloom. The sharp, hard thorns only serve to accent the soft beauty of the rose.

Sing roses into the hearts of the congregation. Turn your sanctuary or auditorium into a rose garden. There is enough pain out there to birth a beautiful bouquet. For some, this time of the year is the very depth of their night. Sing songs of the light. Sing the message of the angels. Sing the good news that the Rose is blooming. Indeed, sing the sleepless to sleep. Sing Mary's lullaby to the baby being born in hearts throughout the congregation. "Lo, how a Rose e'er blooming . . . it [comes] a floweret bright, amid the cold of winter, when half spent [is] the night."

Prayer: Dear God, how precious is the birth of your Son into the dark and frightened hearts of humankind. Help us always to be in touch with his softness and gentle fragrance. It is in the baby's name we pray. Amen.

Christmas

Hymn: "Away in a Manger," stanza 1: "*Away in a manger, no crib for a bed, the little Lord Jesus laid down his sweet head. The stars in the sky looked down where he lay, the little Lord Jesus, asleep on the hay.*" (*Words: Anonymous*)

Babies sleep—a lot. There is, therefore, nothing profound about the baby Jesus sleeping soon after his birth. But we look back at the manger through the lens of his life. We see Jesus asleep in a boat on a stormy lake. We see him tired and in need of rest after preaching, healing, and traveling. The ministry of the Master was laced with rest. And there are our Christmas gifts: salvation, ministry, and rest. Rest is wrapped with the bow of Jesus' closed eyes. The work can wait, or go on without me. I am not personally responsible for healing everyone who needs healing. Though I am called to ministry (lay and clergy alike), I can sleep before the next person or crowd is fed.

Rest is a divine gift, but it is often exchanged for things that look more successful or religious. We exchange the unique gift of being for the more practical gift of doing. Doing fits us better and we think we can get more good out of it.

Jesus came into the world to do a great work. Jesus came into the world "in order that the world might be saved through him" (John 3:17b). Yet, he entered this vast mission field and immediately went to sleep. It was not the sun that looked down on his transition from heaven to earth, it was the stars.

We have been given the gift of rest. Jesus has blessed it. Accept it, open it, and use it with what is left of this Christmas season. Remember, it is the gift that keeps on giving.

Prayer: Dear God, thank you for the gift of your Son. Thank you for the gift of rest. Help me to enjoy these gifts throughout the year. In Jesus' name. Amen.

New Year

Scripture: *"Return, O my soul, to your rest, for the* LORD *has dealt bountifully with you." (Ps. 116:7)*

This time of year is great for putting things back in perspective. The end of the year, Thanksgiving, Advent, Christmas; we look back and look forward and realize that the Lord has dealt bountifully with us. Maybe that's why this time of the year is the best for some and the worst for others.

If we take stock and see that we are, indeed, on the bounty side of the ledger, we should find ways to minister to those who have taken stock and cried. All should be afforded the joy of having their souls returned to rest. When looking back doesn't do it for some, we should try to find ways to help them look forward in hope for a new realization of the Lord's bounty.

Can our singing be "seasoned" by this realignment of our perspective? Can we humbly rejoice with the bountiful and hopefully lean into the future with the empty? The music we sing can facilitate these perspectives to a point, but our voices, faces, and hearts must do the convincing. We can only sing our songs one way at a time. But the Holy Spirit can take our sincere desire to minister and give our songs the needed message as they are being heard. We must allow the Spirit to sing through us. We will become uneasy with ourselves and with one another in the choir if we try to sing to these perspectives in our own strength and wisdom. We must allow the soul of our singing to return to its rest, for it is there that the Lord will deal with it bountifully.

Use this time of year to return your singing and your soul to its place of rest, the peace of knowing that the Holy Spirit blesses into abundance the notes and syllables we are able to project.

Prayer: Dear God, thank you for your many blessings. We especially ask that our singing this season and in the year to come, will be your voice, calling people to your bounty. In Jesus' name. Amen.

Winter
Week 1

Hymn: "For the Fruits of This Creation," stanza 1: "For the plowing, sowing, reaping, silent growth while we are sleeping." (Words by Fred Pratt Green, 1970)

If we need permission to rest, it is surely to be found here: "silent growth while we are sleeping." God is awake and at work while we rest, even while we sleep. Everything that we have given to God is being looked after around the clock because God never sleeps. We can rest. In our line from stanza 1 it is evident that what "we" can do has been done (plowing, sowing) or must wait for God's work to be done (reaping). The part that God does, without us, goes on, even while we rest (silent growth). The outcome is in God's hands. That is true not only while we are asleep, but also while we are awake.

What we know about God's work while we are sleeping should temper how we work in consort with God while we are awake. We do what we can and trust God with the part that only God can do. That's a restful thought to take with us throughout the day's work.

The things we don't give to God may well keep us awake. Our worries and concerns can rob us of rest. Often, it is at night that we worry about the things over which we have no control. We have spent the day working on the things that are in our control to some extent. At night, other, deeper things demand attention. We can give those concerns to our rest time or we can give them to God, who never sleeps and works on the "silent growth while we are sleeping."

There is a related truth in our singing. Our hymns and anthems can help us turn concerns over to God, or we can sing these songs as items on our Wednesday and Sunday "to do" lists. What function will this song serve? Keep responsibility for the answer or give it to God.

A wonderful thing happens when we give the results of our singing and the solution to our problems to God: we are ministered to. In the midst of fulfilling the work and worship for which we are responsible, we minister to one another. Thanks be to God.

Prayer: Dear God, I thank you for your presence and power. Thank you for lifting my burdens, even when I am sleeping. Help me to rely on you as fully while I am awake. In Jesus' name. Amen.

Hymn: *"Jesus Calls Us," stanza 1: "Jesus calls us over the tumult of our life's wild, restless sea; day by day his sweet voice soundeth, saying, 'Christian, follow me!' "* *(Words by Cecil Frances Alexander, 1852)*

It is interesting to me that so many young people entering college and graduating with various degrees are undecided about their first step into their life's work. I don't say that judgmentally, it is simply an intriguing fact. Yet, it isn't all that surprising when we realize that all of us spend a lifetime responding to Jesus' call, "Christian, follow me!" Once we've started on the journey, is it really necessary for us to continue listening for the call? Yes, because we don't know the course of the entire journey when we're taking it one step at a time.

The life that our hymn writer refers to as a restless sea has a tendency to push or pull us off course. Note that it is the Christian to whom Jesus is calling in the song. We need to constantly stay close enough to the Savior to hear "his sweet voice" and its signal call.

The sweet voice of Jesus often sounds through the combined voices of the choir. We must be alert to the voice, hear it for ourselves, so we can emphasize it as we sing. It will always say follow me, but we must listen for its accent in this song, its intensity in the next, its simplicity in the one that follows. Singing the call of Jesus every week will tune our ears to hear it. The next step is ours. We sing the call to the congregation, but we must answer the call for ourselves. The call can be sung, but the answer must be lived. Can we do both?

The call comes in many ways, but to and through the choir is one of the ways. The call comes to many people. The choir's call is to follow Jesus' example of living the message, not just preaching or singing it. The choir hears it, the daily sounding of the quiet inner voice saying, "Christian, follow me!"

Prayer: Dear God, help us to work at living the answer as diligently as we work at singing the call. In Jesus' name. Amen.

Winter
Week 3

Scripture: "He said to them, 'Come away to a deserted place all by your-selves and rest a while.' For many were coming and going and they had no leisure even to eat." (Mark 6:31)

Does that sound familiar? "For many were coming and going and they had no leisure even to eat." It sounds like choir members. The responsibilities of family, work, church in general, and choir specifically combine for a great deal of "coming and going," so much so that there's no time "even to eat."

Good + good + good + good = bad when the total allows no room for rest. You know the dangers of physical, mental, and emotional stress. The dilemma is not new. In our scripture passage for today, Jesus was talking to his stressed-out disciples. Jesus, the one for whom they were working, called them away from the people, their needs, and their demands. "Come away," he said, "to a deserted place all by yourselves and rest a while." That's Jesus talking—the one and only Messiah.

Rest is physical and that is obviously important. Rest is mental and emotional and that is also important. But rest is also spiritual. A practical theology (that is, what your daily actions say you really believe) that says, "I must push until I drop" is a theology that says, "I cannot trust God to take care of things."

Are we to sing of God's all-knowing, mighty power and then live as if God were an employee we can't fully trust? Rest says, first and foremost, "God can take care of things."

"Come away to a deserted place all by yourselves and rest a while." Where might that place be for you? Maybe, practically speaking, it's a time more than a place in your world. But what if it were a place with time? Jesus encourages us to find the place and the time. Go there, rest, and eat at leisure. You may have to explain to some folks that you are not bailing out. Explain that you are simply re-energizing physically, emotionally, and spiritually. If you are accused of bailing out by others or yourself, remember this scripture and let Jesus do your talking.

Prayer: Dear God, help me to find my quiet place and time. Help those who will need to understand, to indeed understand. Refresh my soul, I pray. In Jesus' name. Amen.

Hymn: "*Love Divine, All Loves Excelling,*" *stanza 2:* "*Breathe, O breathe thy loving Spirit into every troubled breast! Let us all in thee inherit; let us find that second rest.*" (*Words by Charles Wesley, 1747*)

Christians have differing doctrines concerning "seconds": second coming, second blessing, and so on. Here the "second" is "second rest." Be that as it may, everyone can agree that now and then we need to "catch our second wind." That is an expression used in specific regions of our country. Others would say, "catch our second breath." Whatever the wording, the message is this—now and then we need to rest and recover.

Theology aside, we have all experienced times of drifting away, of feeling that God is distant. That feeling is a type of fatigue. It may well be a combination of physical and spiritual fatigue. There is a cure—rest! Trying to carry the whole load by ourselves is troubling and tiring. It shrinks our world, narrows our focus, and consumes our time. We can rest from carrying the whole load.

Rest is exhaling. You've heard the troubled exhale; we call it a sigh. It is at those times that we need resuscitation. Charles Wesley knew that and penned for us a last-gasp prayer: "Breathe, O breathe thy loving Spirit into every troubled breast!" The exclamation point puts this prayer in the category of a 911 call. In fact, it is an immediate concern. When we become aware that we have drifted away, it is like our finger telling us that the stove is hot. Pull away! Find a place and time of rest. Pray Charles Wesley's prayer. The rest is promised to us.

Note that Wesley's prayer is in the context of singing about the love of God. Let God catch you and embrace you. Accept the love God offers. Rest in it. Let God lift burdens and breathe God's refreshing Spirit into your life. God has done it before; remember when Adam was just a lump of clay?

Prayer: Dear God, breathe, O breathe your loving Spirit into my troubled breast. Help me find your refreshing rest. In Jesus' name. Amen.

Winter
Week 5

Scripture: "*Discipline your children, and they will give you rest; they will give delight to your heart.*" *(Prov. 29:17)*

Even well-disciplined children can keep you on the go. Obviously, the rest in this proverb is the delight children give to our hearts. That particular kind of rest comes at the end of work. In the context of your congregation's music ministry the work is to be found in children's choirs and in rehearsing and presenting the music that fills your worship experiences. Children learn directly and indirectly. Directly, they learn the songs we teach them. Indirectly, they understand that "our" songs are meaningful to the church community. Therefore, "our" songs are meaningful to them.

Children disciplined in music as a means of expressing their prayer, praise, and testimony "give delight to your heart." We know that they are learning the story through the songs. We know that the story set to music will be with them throughout their lives. How delightful! We can rest in the fact that the church will live beyond our efforts and beyond us.

The transfer of the story through music from your hearts to the hearts of the children should be a matter of focused discipline. Children's choirs are essential, but they are not the only means of passing the story along. When the children see adults in the choir on Sunday mornings, do they see faces they know to be kind and friendly? Do they see themselves as co-ministers, team members, along with the adults in the music ministry of the church?

Sing with your children. Sing their songs as well as yours. Respect their musicianship. Support their efforts. In these ways "discipline your children, and they will give you rest; they will give delight to your heart."

Prayer: Dear God, thank you for the gift of children. Help us to nurture them in your love and through the gospel story. Help us to teach them the discipline of singing. In Jesus' name. Amen.

Winter
Week 6

Hymn: "Blessed Assurance," stanza 3 "Perfect submission, all is at rest; I in my Savior am happy and blest." (Words by Fanny J. Crosby, 1873)

All is at rest? What world did Fanny Crosby live in? All is not at rest in our world. In fact, it is hard to find some aspect of life on this planet that is at rest. All seems to be in turmoil. Actually, all was not at rest in the late nineteenth and early twentieth centuries either. But Fanny knew what she was writing about. All is *subject* to the rest that we experience in our Savior.

Personal, local, national, and global upheavals are unwelcome and unsettling. No one would deny that. But they do not have to be devastating forever. We can rest in the fact that God is in control. Having made that statement, we do not suddenly understand all of the world's insanity, but the rest is available, nonetheless. Death, divorce, terrorist attacks, and economic reversals: these stop us in our tracks. They take our breath away and leave us speechless. But when we are stopped in our tracks, Jesus meets us there and brings the rest of knowing that God is still in control.

Such knowing must be sung. This is the song of the redeemed. All is at rest. My sin, the world's sin, nothing can destroy the love of God. Happy? Not always. Blest? Yes, always. Joyful? Yes, even when the joy of God's salvation must work its way up through pain. The constant presence of the Holy Spirit and the constant availability of divine comfort—these, according to Fanny Crosby, are simply "a foretaste of glory divine," the heavenly Kingdom of God.

I enjoy how I have often heard this hymn sung in African American congregations: slowly, full of blessed assurance, full of rest.

Prayer: Dear God, we are thankful that the whole world is in your hands, especially since there is so much about this world that we do not understand. Grant us your peace and rest, in Jesus' name. Amen.

Winter
Week 7

Hymn: "My Hope Is Built," stanza 2: "When darkness veils his lovely face, I rest on his unchanging grace." (Words by Edward Mote, 1834)

There isn't much around us that is unchanging. That is a bit unsettling. Faith, love, and trust are often withheld because we do not want things that deep and important to fail or change. All else is subject to change, why should we believe those foundations will never quiver? We may even reserve some of our commitment toward the messages of the hymns and anthems we sing. We'll sing them, but we are not so sure we will, in actual practice, put our whole self into them. The messages of unchanging grace sound good, especially when set to music, but are they true? Are they always true?

We must have hope in order to get up and step into the day. However small it is, hope must be present for us to function. We build that hope on something. Those who build their hope on the stock market will be let down, measurably so. Those who build their hope on military might and strategy may well feel like the elephant frightened by the mouse. Nevertheless these and many other human endeavors are the foundations for many people's hope. These foundations are easily shaken.

Then comes the quiet, persistent song: "My hope is built on nothing less than Jesus' blood and righteousness." Slow, quiet, relentless, the message of the song holds us up, even when its simplicity amazes us. "When darkness veils his lovely face, I rest on his unchanging grace." Solid, consistent, reliable, true. "On Christ the solid rock I stand, all other ground is sinking sand." What? "All other ground is sinking sand." The song continues, turning on the light in the dark place in our heart.

Unceasing, unchanging, "I rest on his unchanging grace" and the Spirit does its quiet work. We are strengthened with renewed hope. We can rest.

Prayer: Dear God, your unconditional love and unchanging grace are the source of our rest. We do, indeed, rest in you. Accept the thanks of our quieted hearts. In Jesus' name. Amen.

Winter
Week 8

Hymn: "Only Trust Him," stanza 1: "Come, every soul by sin oppressed, there's mercy with the Lord; and he will surely give you rest, by trusting in his Word." (Words by John H. Stockton, 1874)

Trust is the basis of just about all that is good in life. Breaking a trust is a serious matter. Such a break is difficult, if not impossible, to mend. Yet we must place our trust in ideas, products, and people every day. Sometimes the trust is so sure we don't even think about it. Sometimes we trust because we have no other choice.

To be deemed trustworthy is one of life's highest honors. It takes time to earn that title and even then it is fragile. One incident can destroy trust that has been built up over a lifetime.

John H. Stockton challenges us to place our trust in God's Word. Read the hymn carefully. He is calling us to place our trust in Jesus, the Living Word, the Word made flesh. Jesus will give us rest. He gives mercy to the oppressed. Everyone is oppressed spiritually by sin. Beyond that many in our world are oppressed physically and emotionally. That oppression is also caused by sin, not their own, but the sin of the oppressors. Political and economic oppression push people down and out into the margins of life. We are admonished by scripture to remember the poor, to give cups of water, to feed and clothe, to heal and lift up the oppressed. We are also told that we will always have the poor with us. Is that a reason to ignore them or the reason to be continually fair and generous? It certainly is reason to turn to Jesus.

The teachings and sacrifice of Jesus are the source of mercy for the oppressed. Again, as Christians and choir members, we are called to both sing and live the truth that "there's mercy with the Lord." We might well find rest from the rush and work of our over-scheduled lives "by trusting in his Word."

"Live simply," the bumper sticker says, "so that others may simply live." Such living will help bring mercy to the oppressed.

Prayer: Dear God, thank you for your mercy that forgives us of our sin. Help us, now, live the mercy as we minister to the oppressed. Help us tell the good news of Jesus and live the good news of plenty for the world. In Jesus' name. Amen.

33

Winter
Week 9

Scripture: *"Then they seized him and led him away, bringing him into the high priest's house. But Peter was following at a distance. When they had kindled a fire in the middle of the courtyard and sat down together, Peter sat among them. Then a servant-girl, seeing him in the firelight, stared at him and said, 'This man also was with him.' "* *(Luke 22:54-56)*

There is "rest" that really isn't rest at all. It is rest that denies the Prince of Peace. Sitting around a campfire should have been restful for Peter, but it wasn't.

We cannot manufacture our own rest. We can bring ourselves to a state of inactivity, but rest isn't quite that easy. Sitting around a campfire or fireplace looks restful and often is, but we can peacefully stare into a fire while volcanoes of fear, worry, and doubt erupt in our hearts.

When we follow Jesus at a distance we have to work harder at finding rest. Inactivity not only fails to bring rest, it often increases the intensity of the volcano. Therefore, we stay active and busy ourselves, denying the power of the Prince of Peace and believing that rest can be found somewhere in the deeper fury of the fire.

After Jesus' Crucifixion and Resurrection, there was to be another campfire experience for Peter. This time, instead of following at a distance, Peter rushed (actually swam) to get closer to Jesus. The campfire was aflame as Jesus prepared the meal of the new dawn. After breakfast, Peter bared his soul to the Prince of Peace. The volcano became dormant. Sitting around the fire was again restful.

"This man also *was* with him"—no rest. "Lord, you know that I love you" (John 21:15)—observe the rest.

Prayer: Lord Jesus, keep us close and open to you. Grant us the courage to stay close and the courage to admit that we have been following from a distance. Let us rest in your presence. In Jesus' name. Amen.

Hymn: *"Dear Lord and Father of Mankind," stanza 4: "And let our ordered lives confess the beauty of thy peace." (Words by John Greenleaf Whittier, 1872)*

Rests create ordered music. Rest creates ordered lives. We are invited to rest in the Lord and then to let our ordered lives confess the beauty of God's peace. Like ordered lives, ordered music speaks of the beauty of God's peace, the beauty of discipline, and involvement under control.

Some people feel that new age music is peaceful. I find it disconcerting. As soothing as it may be at the outset, a few minutes into it I begin to wonder where this drifting is headed. Will it ever end? That question is second only to the more troubling concern of "How will this end?" Ordered, disciplined music is peaceful to me. Structure and a sense of direction allow me to give myself to the beauty of the music. *That* is peaceful.

Even rousing, exuberant music is under control—the rests tell us so. It's rather like tapping the breaks on your car on a long downhill slope. You don't want to stop yet, but it's good to be reassured that you can. The little interruption brings a sense of peace and well-being and allows you to enjoy the beauty of the scenery.

Moments of rest, even when you can't stop yet, are reassuring. They bring to mind the beauty of peace, the rejuvenation of deeper rest to come.

Every Sunday, the choir has the opportunity and responsibility to minister to the congregation by demonstrating that life can be lived under control. For some, the good news will be that life can get *back* under control. That is a beautiful, encouraging, and peaceful thought. Our music outlines the reassuring message of the rests.

Prayer: Dear God, it is our prayer that our ordered lives would confess the beauty of your peace. So we pray our ordered music. Sing through us the assurance of your presence and ultimate control. In Jesus' name. Amen.

Winter
Week 11

Scripture: "Be still, and know that I am God! I am exalted among the nations, I am exalted in the earth." (Ps. 46:10)

It can happen in rehearsal, it can happen in worship. The final chord and word is held, then the cutoff—then a silence that can only be described as a holy hush. This is very much a rest. It is a transitional rest. We are transitioning from the Kingdom of Heaven back into the kingdom of this world, from music to the spoken word, from what will be to what is. That is why the silence at the end of an especially moving anthem is so holy. It is rest.

Perhaps *transformation* is a better word than *transition* for describing what happens in this special rest. In those pregnant seconds of silence at the end of the wonderful anthem, we know that Jesus is about to be born to us again. We know that we will not face life in the same way we would have just a few minutes and measures earlier. In that special moment we are being still and are full of the knowledge that God is, indeed, God. We have visited that place in our heart and being that is full of God's presence, a place that perhaps we had been ignoring. The music has taken us to that place. The immediate and intense silence that follows can only be described as what we hear in God's words through the psalmist: "Be still, and know that I am God!" God's words became our road map and when we got to our destination, God was waiting for us.

Not every anthem ends in this holy hush, this rest between worlds. But, when the moments do come and everyone knows instinctively to be still, God is exalted among all the nations and among worlds we may not know. God is exalted in our world. When we come out of that holy hush we are different. We will, then, be significantly, even if slightly, different people in our world. Observing the rest at the end of the transforming anthem is a high and holy act of worship. Choir members are priests at that moment, perhaps more than at any other time.

Prayer: Dear God, help us to be open to your embrace at the end of the anthem and in the other moments of rest in our lives. We do, indeed, want to be still and know that you are God. In Jesus' name. Amen.

Scripture: "*And he said to them, 'Why are you afraid, you of little faith?' Then he got up and rebuked the winds and the sea; and there was a dead calm."* (Matt. 8:26)

The sea was in turmoil. The surface of the water was busy, angry, and storm-tossed. Waves were pushing the disciples around and crashing into their boat. They were frightened by the storm and upset with Jesus for sleeping through it. When Jesus woke he scolded the disciples, the wind, and the sea as if they were arguing children. When Jesus resumed his rest, the disciples asked one another just what sort of man Jesus was. *Who and what did we just observe here?* They had observed the Prince of Peace at rest. Sleep doesn't come any deeper than that.

The choir is permeated with the Prince of Peace. He created, gifted, and called each choir member to lead in worship. Jesus is the example for our lives and the subject of our worship. He is in the boat with us. In a very real sense, the choir is called upon to help the congregation deal with their fears, their questions about what sort of man Jesus is, and just exactly what we are observing when we look to Jesus as our example. But frightened people have a hard time convincing others to be calm in the midst of their storms.

Several years ago on a flight from Kansas City to Memphis we experienced the worst turbulence I have ever flown through. The flight was not long, but the storm made it feel like an eternity. The darkness of the night exaggerated the lightning. I was sitting in the forward-most seat, next to the bulkhead. I was facing the flight attendant, who was strapped into her seat more securely than the passengers. She was frightened. She did not even attempt to appear calm or to reassure her passengers. She would not have been very convincing if she had tried.

Choir members are human and experience the same turbulence as the congregation. But we have an obligation to remember that the Prince of Peace is in the boat with us. Choir, sing into the storms—yours and theirs. The song is needed every Sunday.

Prayer: Our prayer to you, dear God the Son, is that we will constantly be aware of your presence. Help us then, to rest in you and lead others to your calm during the storms. In Jesus' name. Amen.

Spring
Week 1

Hymn: "This Is a Day of New Beginnings," stanza 1: "This is a day of new beginnings, time to remember and move on, time to believe what love is bringing, laying to rest the pain that's gone." (Words by Brian Wren, 1978)

Brian Wren's hymn reminds us of the freshness of baptism and communion. At this time of year our calendars, secular and liturgical, also speak to us of freshness. New beginnings are important. They are times for us to focus on "laying to rest the pain that's gone." Forgiveness is a wonderful gift. It is a costly gift. Forgiving others and ourselves is difficult. Accepting God's forgiveness is also difficult. In fact, all this forgiving is interrelated. Still, forgiveness remains a precious gift. Still, forgiveness remains a costly gift.

The cost is declared every time we see a cross. It is the symbol of just how costly the gift of forgiveness is. To reject forgiveness is to reject the cross. We are told to take up our cross daily. That scripture is not talking about our sore knees. It is talking about the symbol of forgiveness. Brian Wren has given us the song of the new day and its cross: "Time to remember and move on." Remember what? For me it is to remember forgiveness: God's forgiveness of my sin, my forgiving others, asking forgiveness from others. "Time to remember and move on." What a refreshing thought, to move on into the new day and its clean slate.

Sing this song into your own soul and then sing it into the congregation. Give them the chance to remember and move on. Sing the freshness of forgiveness. What a ministry for you and the choir to participate in! New beginnings—there is nothing more invigorating. There is nothing that speaks more eloquently, more enthusiastically, about the beauty of life. "This is a day of new beginnings." Is this not the gospel?

Now is the "time to believe what love is bringing, laying to rest the pain that's gone." Sing into the congregation, the cure for their pain.

Prayer: Dear God, thank you for the gift of new beginnings. Help me to embrace the new beginnings that you and I know are needed in my life. In Jesus' name. Amen.

Spring

Hymn: "Go Now in Peace": "May the love of God surround you every-where, everywhere you may go." (Words by Natalie Sleeth, 1976)

Peace is portable rest. In my seminary office, I have a small fountain on my desk, and my desk chair is a rocking chair. When both are in motion I can take little thirty-second "vacations." The combination is very peaceful, but the chair and the fountain are not conveniently portable. However, they produce rest "to go." In any class or meeting, I can remember the rocking chair and the fountain that await me back in my office. The resulting peace is refresh-ing rest.

Natalie Sleeth's little musical benediction restores in us aware-ness that the love of God does, indeed, surround us everywhere we may go. There is great peace in knowing that we are sur-rounded by God's love and that peace is portable. We do not have to remember and return to a place of peace—the person of peace is always with us. Rest is always within reach.

There is an interesting phenomenon related to my office chair and fountain: they put visitors at peace and rest, as well. When we are in our place of peace, those around us sense it and join us. It is true in offices with rocking chairs and fountains and it is true in the sphere of the surrounding love of God. What a wonderful thought that people might find rest by simply being near us, because we have learned to observe the rest provided by God's peace within us.

Enter the choir loft and lead in worship fully aware that you are surrounded by the love of God. It can bring rest to the weary souls in the congregation. Remember, it is portable. Let the love of God surround you everywhere you may go in your restless week.

Prayer: Dear God, grant us your peace so that we might bring rest to those around us, both now and throughout the week. In Jesus' name. Amen.

Spring
Week 3

Hymn: "For All the Saints," stanza 1: "For all the saints, who from their labors rest, who thee by faith before the world confessed, thy name, O Jesus, be forever blest. Alleluia, Alleluia!" (Words by William W. How, 1864)

It's a strange kind of rest: stopping to remember those "saints who from their labors rest," who "before the world confessed" the name of Jesus. You know who they are. They are the persons whose very lives confessed that Jesus is Lord. You know who they are because their lives touched yours. Even though they have gone on to heaven, the very remembrance of them refreshes your soul; you rest in their memory. Perhaps there were people like that in your choir.

How does one attain such status in the memory of others? How does one move from a name chiseled in granite to a spirit engrained on the heart of someone other than family? I think it has something to do with bringing a certain refreshing into the lives of others. They can rest in your friendship. That's the kind of relationship choir members should have with one another. It is the kind of relationship choir members should have with the congregation. When our lives confess Jesus as Lord, our relationships become a place of rest for the anthems we sing.

In the end, we thank Jesus for the saints who have blessed our lives. They were and are a blessing to us. Their lives should challenge us to live similar lives. Thinking about them, we take a rest from our self-focused achieving, surviving, and obtaining.

Take a moment to remember "all the saints" in your experience. Rest in the inspiration you gain from simply remembering them. Then listen to how this bit of rest energizes the anthems you sing.

Prayer: Thank you God, for the rest we find in remembering the dear souls who have ministered to us and encouraged us throughout our lives. Help others to see Jesus in us, for it is in his name we pray. Amen.

Scripture: "*I will both lie down and sleep in peace; for you alone, O Lord, make me lie down in safety.*" (Ps. 4:8)

Surely we've all seen it—a choir member sound asleep in the choir loft on Sunday morning. As awkward as that may be, there's something about it that I rather like. Christians are citizens of the kingdom of heaven. We are simply passing through the kingdom of this world. Therefore, when we are with brothers and sisters in Christ, in the choir loft, in the sanctuary, on Sunday morning, involved in worship, we are as much "at home" as we are ever going to be on earth. There's nothing quite like a nap on the couch at home, safely surrounded by family and familiarity.

Please know that I am not advocating a fifth section in the choir—sopranos, altos, tenors, basses, and snore-ers. But the choir, even with all its work, should be, at least spiritually, a place of rest. It is here that we sing the songs of home. It is here that we sing the songs of God's love. It is here that we sing the songs of ultimate safety. Thanks to the texts we sing in our many anthems, choir members know as much as or more than anyone else why Christians should "lie down and sleep in peace." We sing the truth of God's love and strength over and over again. Every anthem we sing is an echo of Psalm 37: "Rest in the Lord" (v. 7*a* KJV).

But the rest that we enjoy, and of which we sing, is not meant for the choir alone. Wake up, for we sing in the presence of and on behalf of a congregation of tired and troubled people. We sing to the Lord, who can "make [us] lie down in safety." Tell the congregation that there is rest, that they can "both lie down and sleep in peace" and that their safe rest is the work of the Lord alone.

Enjoy a great nap on Sunday . . . afternoon.

Prayer: Dear God, we join our brother, St. Francis of Assisi, and ask that we might be instruments of your peace. Through our singing, soothe the hearts of your people toward rest. In Jesus' name. Amen.

Spring
Week 5

Hymn: "This Is My Father's World," stanza 1: "This is my Father's world, and to my listening ears all nature sings, and round me rings the music of the spheres. This is my Father's world: I rest me in the thought of rocks and trees, of skies and seas; his hand the wonders wrought." (Words by Maltbie D. Babcock, 1901)

It can happen in your backyard. It can happen in a national park. It's a matter of focus. As Christians, we know not to worship nature. But we have allowed ourselves to ignore nature's testimony to the God we *do* worship.

Among the many things I have learned from my wife over the last thirty years is the discipline of seeing God. She is a talented amateur photographer. Driving down a road or walking down a path, when she says, "Stop," it's a call to worship. Like an altar boy assisting a priest, I silently hand her tripods, lenses, and film; all the while out of the corner of my eye trying to find the icon before she points her camera at it. I said "silently" and that is true now. There was a time when, checking to see if I had guessed right, I would say, "Ooo, look at that," or "Wow, there's a great shot."

She bought me a camera one Father's Day. Now, after my silent acolyte duties, I quietly look through my camera at "rocks and trees," at "skies and seas" and see the testimonies that "his hand the wonders wrought." Looking through the camera's lens has focused the eye of my soul. Camera or not, I see "shots" that stop me in my tracks for a moment of worship.

The interesting part of all this is that sharpening the focus of my eye has also sharpened the focus of my ear. Now "to my listening ears all nature sings, and round me rings the music of the spheres." Things I see and things I hear often call me to rest. And by observing these rests, I am reminded again that it is "his hand the wonders wrought."

Along your path, take time to rest, even for a moment. Observe, in the details of your surroundings, the beautiful evidence of the Creator's presence and love.

Prayer: Dear God, thank you for moments of rest in a busy day. Thank you for providing us with glimpses of your beauty in art and intricacies, in nature and in smiles. In Jesus' name. Amen.

Scripture: *"For with you is the fountain of life; in your light we see light." (Ps. 36:9)*

There is a fountain in the courtyard of the seminary where I teach. It is a gentle fountain, a peaceful font. It does not dance or show off. It bubbles. The source of the bubbling is located deep in the pool. It is a place where I can take long trips in the span of just a few minutes as I sit on the surrounding benches. The trips are retreats, wading into solitude. Even the occasional birds that visit the fountain for a drink while I am there seem to know that I should not be disturbed. They, too, have come for refreshing. We leave one another alone.

Even though the fountain doesn't dance, light does. The slow deep bubbling that keeps the water fresh and attracts the birds also causes the light to dance. Flashes of light that I would not otherwise have seen, reach out to remind me that while life may be deep and barely rippling, the Light is dancing over me and around me with extravagance and joy. Life is bubbling and Light is dancing and all to the quiet accompaniment of a gentle fountain.

I have sat on those benches for as little as fifteen minutes and for as long as a couple of hours. The longer the better, but even short periods of time there are refreshing. In fact, I can walk down the hallways of windows and peer out at the fountain as I rush to class or to a meeting. A quick glance observes the rest that I know is there and my soul calms down a bit. I make a mental note to get back out there as soon as I can.

In a very real sense, spending time in prayer and reading the Bible are like visiting a slowly bubbling fountain and its flashes of light. God and God's Word are always there, always refreshing, always the source of a new bit of light. The anthems we sing in choir are like walks down the window-lined hallway. They allow us to see the fountain. Next time you catch one of those quick glances, determine to visit the fountain as soon as possible.

Prayer: Dear God, help us to remember that you are the fountain of life and the light of the world. You bring depth to our shallowness, quenching to our thirst, and light to our darkness. Sing through us your refreshing, bubbling peace. In Jesus' name. Amen.

Spring
Week 7

Hymn: "I'll Praise My Maker While I've Breath," stanza 3: "The Lord pours eyesight on the blind; the Lord supports the fainting mind and sends the laboring conscience peace. God helps the stranger in distress, the widow and the fatherless, and grants the prisoner sweet release." (Words by Isaac Watts, 1719)

Everyone has to "work through" something to go about his or her daily responsibilities. Physical challenges, emotional or mental affliction, guilt, loneliness, loss, imprisonment—everyone wrestles with something that pulls backward every time they take a step forward. Most of the people we see each day are pulling some kind of a weight behind them. Church-going, choir-singing Christians are no exception.

Getting to choir rehearsal is a major accomplishment on some days. Singing in the choir, on some Sunday mornings, seems like the height of hypocrisy. Yet, the Lord pours out grace and strength. We are reminded of that twice a week as we sing songs of testimony to God's presence and provision and find ourselves a bit more refreshed than we were an hour ago. If the songs we rehearse and then sing in worship revitalize us, they can do the same for those who listen. On Sunday mornings we sing the eyesight the Lord would pour on the blind, the support the Lord would pour on the fainting mind, the peace the Lord would pour on the laboring conscience, the friendship the Lord would pour on the stranger in distress, the comfort the Lord would pour on the widow and the fatherless, the sweet release the Lord would pour on the prisoner, whatever constitutes their prison.

We experience grace upon grace when we allow God to sing such blessings into the hearts and lives of the congregation through the songs that bless us while we sing. In fact, we singers are granted sweet release as we sing the good news of the gospel. There are good reasons to praise our Maker while we've breath—even if it seems like our last one.

Prayer: Dear God, thank you for giving us the talent to sing, a message to proclaim, and a ministry to perform. Grant us the strength and vision of ministry to keep coming back week after week. In Jesus' name. Amen.

Scripture: "For God's foolishness is wiser than human wisdom, and God's weakness is stronger than human strength." (1 Cor. 1:25)

Need a place to rest? Here are a couple of suggestions: God's wisdom and God's strength. If you see yourself in every representation of Hercules carrying the world on his shoulders, you need to take a load off. God is the Creator of that world and yours. All the sculptures and paintings I have seen show Hercules bent over. Such a burden will crush mere mortals like us. The strength and wisdom of God are no myth. The African American spiritual tells us that he's got the whole world in his *hands*. I get the mental picture of God with a blue and green beach ball.

Every week we sing songs that in one way or another declare God's strength and wisdom. This is an important ministry. Sing the mighty power of God and watch giant globes come rolling down the aisles. Are we afraid that our concerns are too small for God to consider? Well, according to our scripture passage, even if God takes them lightly we need not worry. God's foolishness is wiser than our wisdom. Are we afraid that our burdens are too lightweight for the one who knows the gravity of the universe? The apostle Paul, under the inspiration of the Holy Spirit, assures us that even God's weakness is stronger than our strength.

We can become completely worn out from constantly testing our own strength. We need to rest. We can end up simply becoming aware of what we don't know and don't understand by constantly relying on our own wisdom. We need to rest. In scripture and in song we hear God patiently saying, "Come unto me and rest."

As you rehearse the music in your choir folder this week, watch for testimonies of God's strength and wisdom. When you sing in worship on Sunday, be aware that you are telling the good news that the One for whom creating planets was no more demanding than creating sand, loves them. God's grace is tougher than human sin.

Prayer: Dear God, forgive us when our actions show that we doubt your wisdom and strength. Guide us and strengthen us, we pray. In Jesus' name. Amen.

Spring
Week 9

Hymn: "Marching to Zion," stanza 3: "The hill of Zion yields a thousand sacred sweets before we reach the heavenly fields, or walk the golden streets." (Words by Isaac Watts, 1707)

The church is in an uphill struggle. Indeed, Watts has reminded us in another hymn that this vile world is not a friend to grace. The values of the kingdom of this world and the kingdom of heaven are opposites. To bring people into the kingdom of heaven is to turn their world upside down. We know that because we are constantly struggling to "do it right," to be more Christlike in a world that pushes servants down in its rush to the success at the top. Being a Christ-follower makes one a rather peculiar person. This world is not our home, we're just passing through and the path often seems very steep. But Watts reminds us "the hill of Zion yields a thousand sacred sweets."

There are many sweet moments, events, and people along the way—thousands of them. It is important from time to time to stop, exhale, rest, and remember. Remember the people who have helped you and enriched your life. Remember the times of joy and accomplishment you have experienced with your congregation. Remember the moments of laughter or crying with dear friends; moments that stay in your memory as warm, breathing photographs. We have not yet reached the heavenly fields or set foot on the golden streets, but we get glimpses of heaven now and then.

Such thoughts keep us marching. While you're marching, watch for moments in the making. Know that the next conversation, the next committee project, the next worship service or concert could be one of the sweets that you and others will think back on a little further up the hill. Such sweets are sacred. God gives them, blesses them, and calls them to remembrance. Keep marching, keep singing, keep Sabbath; that is, take time to rest and remember.

Prayer: Dear God, thank you for the people and the moments that have blessed my life and continue to be a source of encouragement and inspiration. Help me to be open to your leadership in my life so that I might be one of those people or a part of one of those moments for someone else. In Jesus' name. Amen.

Spring
Week 10

Hymn: "Holy, Holy, Holy! Lord God Almighty," stanza 1: "Holy, holy, holy! Lord God Almighty! Early in the morning our song shall rise to thee. Holy, holy, holy! Merciful and mighty, God in three persons, blessed Trinity!" (Words by Reginald Heber, 1826)

Mornings are a great time to raise our songs to God, but we don't have to wait for morning. Whenever we take the time to pause and focus on God, to pray, praise, and listen, it is the dawning of a "new day." Sometimes we need to pray: "Lord, my day needs a new start." In fact, by the time you get to that point God already knows that things are in a mess and is waiting for you to hand it over.

The song we raise to God in these times of darkness before the dawn may be a song of desperation, or loneliness, or fear. Even those songs have a way of turning into songs of praise as the burdens lift and light starts to seep in a few little beams at a time. I once heard a dentist say that he could not understand why people put up with toothaches when relief is so readily available. I wonder the same thing about Christians who put up with living in spiritual darkness.

Our songs of impromptu dawning may be songs of joy. Successful completion of a task, a wonderful surprise, an unexpected compliment; these are moments of joy that need to be shared. Why not share them with the Source? Raise them in silent song to the holy Lord God Almighty.

The songs we raise in a midday dawning may be prayers of concern for a loved one. These prayer songs usher in the dawn of hope. Each one of us is just one person, but we can pray to the one God in three persons who knows the situation's or person's past, present, and future. Raising our songs to God is raising the burden to God. God is merciful and mighty. It doesn't get any better or more hopeful than that.

The God of eternal day is a never-ending source of dawning. Raise your prayers and songs to God and find yourself early in a new morning. Awake to the Comforter's presence feeling rested.

Prayer: Dear God, burdens can be crushing and night can seem endless. The darkness almost has a personality. Come lift and lighten. I give my burdens to you in Jesus' name. Amen.

Spring
Week 11

Scripture: "The LORD is my shepherd, I shall not want. He makes me lie down in green pastures; he leads me beside still waters; he restores my soul." (Ps. 23:1-3a)

The psalmist was observing a time of rest. God had guided him to the time and place of rest and the psalmist knew it. Green pastures, still water—the Lord used these simple wonders of nature to restore the psalmist's soul. Does *your* Lord ever lead you to rest or demand that you keep working, ever harder, ever faster? You may not be serving the same God the psalmist served. Is it possible that the one true God, the psalmist's Lord, is, spiritually speaking, sitting under a tree in some green pasture, near a gentle stream with a picnic basket, waiting for you to get off work?

There aren't many gods who grant their subjects rest. Success doesn't. Pride doesn't. Greed doesn't. Guilt doesn't. These "little g" gods are ruthless and uncaring. They don't lead to green pastures. They lead their sheep to the slaughterhouse.

Some Christians see the Lord as stern, angry, and demanding. Their songs convey orders and deadlines and ultimatums. If they ever lie down in green pastures it would be to seek a vantage point to observe those who might come to the still waters for a drink. Some of their songs are based on psalms, but they save this psalm, and others like it, to bury those who die in battle. For them the only rest is the final rest.

I believe the Lord, our God, walks through the green pastures and beside the still waters and grieves when they are turned into battlegrounds. God calls us to rest, to restore our souls. There is risk in rest. Someone might get ahead of us. Someone might sneak up on us. Something might not get done today. Still, the Lord *makes* me lie down in green pastures, like a parent whose child is resisting a nap. In so doing, he restores my soul.

Whole notes, whole rests, release from syncopation: Rest. Rest for the soul, rest for creation, rest from fighting, rest from "doing," rest for the weary; observe the rests, it will restore your soul.

Prayer: Dear God, I'm tired. It seems I work all the time. I even work for you, especially at rehearsal and on Sunday mornings. Please lead me to the green pastures and still waters of Sabbath. In Jesus' name. Amen.

Good Friday

Hymn: "What Wondrous Love Is This," stanza 1: "What wondrous love is this, O my soul! What wondrous love is this that caused the Lord of bliss to bear the dreadful curse for my soul." (Words: USA folk hymn)

This reminds us of a hymn we considered earlier in the year, "What Child Is This?" One of the differences, however, is that this hymn has no question marks. There are no question marks to be found in our singing of it or in the truth of it. This hymn is a statement of deepest love. The Lord of bliss has born our dreadful curse—O my soul. What are we to say? What are we to do? How are we to live?

It is right to pause in wonder, humility, and awe. The One who was without sin, hangs nailed to a cross, holding in his being all the shame, guilt, and grief of all our sin. What wondrous love is this!

Prayer: On this day, think on these things, rest from words, and let your prayer be silent.

Easter

Hymn: "Alleluia," stanza 1: "Alleluia." (Words by Jerry Sinclair in this one song—and by angels and Christians everywhere in thousands of other songs)

At long last, we get to sing "Alleluia." And I am not necessarily referring to the long forty days of Lent. I am referring to that seeming eternity between Maundy Thursday and Easter Sunday morning.

It's bad enough having to refrain from using the word "alleluia" throughout Lent and focusing on sacrifice, but it is harder still to hear the words "Our Lord is dead." There are many free-church traditions that simply will not say it. I understand. It's tough. It tastes like blasphemy on its way out of the mouth. It sounds like blasphemy when it reaches the ears. But it was true for three days. And we feel the pain and emptiness of that truth when we say it and hear it.

But then comes Sunday and we are refreshed, renewed, and re-energized with one simple word: "Alleluia!" The word is so powerful we wrap it in the wonderful announcement: "He is risen! He is risen indeed!" What a prelude to the one word that fits all Christian traditions in all languages on earth and in heaven: "Alleluia."

Sing it with all your heart. Sing it with tears of joy. Sing it in the face of death. Sing its light into the darkness. Sing "Alleluia!"

In many congregations the children are given little bells as they enter the sanctuary on Easter Sunday morning. Their assignment is to listen for the word "Alleluia." Every time they hear it they are to ring their bells. It is delightful and joyful.

Sing and live your alleluia. Ring the bells of heaven.

Prayer: Dear God, thank you for the joy of Easter. Thank you for Jesus' victory and for the hope it brings. Thank you for the light of your love and salvation. In Jesus' name. Alleluia and Amen!

Hymn: *"Jesus, the Very Thought of Thee,'"* stanza 1: *"Jesus, the very thought of thee with sweetness fills the breast; but sweeter far thy face to see, and in thy presence rest."* (Words attributed to Bernard of Clairvaux, 12th cent.)

We must never lose sight of the true source and end of our singing. The choir's anthems and the congregational songs in which we participate are, in one way or another, heaven songs. We sing toward heaven, eyes fixed on the heavenly rest at the end of the earthly journey. That's because "this world is not our home." Whatever our earthly citizenship, we are first and foremost citizens of the kingdom of heaven.

Jesus makes our citizenship and its songs possible. Jesus is the brother sent to bring us to our kingdom home. He is constantly reminding us of the warmth of that home and gently guides us in that direction. He reminds us how we are to behave on our way to our kingdom home and how to connect with this world without becoming attached to it.

The Bible records Jesus' comments about heaven and John's vision of heaven, but we still don't know much about the beauty and glory of the place. But through the scripture passages, our songs, and the Holy Spirit, we get occasional spiritual whiffs and glimpses of what awaits. The top of the anticipation list is the fact that we will be with Jesus.

He came from heaven to live among us. He lived and taught life-lessons that continue to enrich our living. He died for us. He arose and returned to heaven to prepare a place for us. The Servant is the King of Kings. Bernard of Clairvaux thought on these things and his heart overflowed with the love-note, "Jesus, the very thought of thee with sweetness fills the breast; but sweeter far thy face to see, and in thy presence rest." His eyes, heart, mind, and words were fixed on Jesus. He lived here focused on the rest there and it affected his very being: his speech, work, and relationships.

Notice that the words are "attributed" to Bernard of Clairvaux. That means he might have written them, but, even if he didn't, he could have. Can that be said of us? He might have said that. I might have learned that from her. But even if he or she didn't say that or do that wonderful thing, they could have. Keeping our hearts and minds focused on Jesus will cause us to glow with the attributes of Jesus.

Prayer: Dear God, help my words and actions be attributed to Jesus. It is in his name I pray. Amen.

Hymn: *"Glorious Things of Thee Are Spoken," stanza 1: "On the Rock of Ages founded, what can shake thy sure repose?" (Words by John Newton, 1779)*

I love these kinds of rhetorical questions: "Who shall separate us from the love of God?" "If God be for us, who can be against us?" "What can shake thy sure repose?" The answers? No one can separate us, no one can be against us, and nothing can shake our repose. The statements sing with faith and resolve and certainty. We sing them in the face of adversity. We sing them in defiance of disappointment and setbacks. Then after choir rehearsal or worship, we get in our cars, drive home, and worry about work, bills, and family all the way home. I call upon another rhetorical question: "What's wrong with this picture?"

We cannot, nor should we, abandon our responsibilities. We can, however, and should, rest from our worry. Prayer, asking for advice or help, doing what we can do today, in the context of this day, and watching for God's solution to come together piece by piece can be restful. At least these can lead to more satisfying rest. When these steps are taken under the leadership of the Holy Spirit, and in the confidence of God's presence, the moments and hours of the day become times of rest in our sure repose that cannot be shaken.

Our hymn speaks of salvation. Our sure repose is effective immediately. The Rock on which our deep hope and rest is founded cannot be shaken. It can be attacked, but not breached. Glorious things are spoken about our God and the salvation God makes available for us. One of the most glorious is that our sure repose is solid, at peace because no warfare can defeat it. Warfare can come, and too often does come. Attacks are often formidable. Storms are often frightening. But the truth that is so solid it can be expressed in a question stands firm: "On the Rock of Ages founded, what can shake thy sure repose?"

Newton's first stanza ends with these words, "With salvation's walls surrounded, thou mayst smile at all thy foes."

Prayer: Dear God, restore to us the joy, the peace, and the rest of your salvation. In Jesus' name. Amen.

Summer
Week 3

Scripture: "*Come to me, all you that are weary and are carrying heavy burdens, and I will give you rest. Take my yoke upon you, and learn from me; for I am gentle and humble in heart, and you will find rest for your souls. For my yoke is easy, and my burden is light.*" (Matt. 11:28-30)

"All you that are weary and carrying heavy burdens"—do you know anyone who doesn't fit that description? "Weary" is a familiar and disturbingly descriptive word. "Carrying heavy burdens" paints the picture of many in our society, no doubt many in your choir and congregation. Calendars and credit cards with no "white space" are heavy burdens. Terrorism and the declared war on terrorism make us weary because we see no end to either. Children are kidnapped out of their own homes and billion dollar businesses fail seemingly overnight. We are a weary people.

Jesus says to the world, "Come to me, all you that are weary . . . and I will give you rest." Yet, even we who love him and follow him try to find another way to be comforted. Often, it is to go deeper into the excesses that caused the weariness in the first place. It is as if we were yoked to the pace and the pattern of the world. In contrast, Jesus' yoke is easy. His burden is light.

Echoing through our hearts and minds are the sounds of Handel's *Messiah*—the oratorio we sung at Christmas returns to minister to us now. "His yoke is easy, his burden is light, is light." The melismas bounce along the surface—light, airy. This is our ministry of music at work. This is scriptural truth flying free to the hearts that need it, available to any and all who sang it or heard it. The words of the gentle, humble Savior search us out. They find us and call to us. Your singing matters for it carries the words of Jesus. Sing. Get the words right, get the notes right. Sing, for the songs you sing minister to your heart and then soar out into the weary and heavily burdened congregation.

"Learn from me; for I am gentle and humble in heart, and you will find rest for your souls." Is that the answer to weariness and being overburdened—taking Jesus' yoke, being gentle and humble in heart, like Jesus? If so, we have some more singing to do. We must sing ourselves and our congregations out of the yoke of the kingdom of this world and into the yoke of "the kingdom of our

Lord and of his Christ." Then we will find rest for our souls and those in the congregation.

Prayer: Dear God, forgive us for ignoring the call and the yoke of the Savior. Forgive the sin of sustained weariness. Help us to accept your deliverance from our overburdened lives. In Jesus' name. Amen.

Summer
Week 4

Hymn: *"To God Be the Glory," stanza 2: "The vilest offender who truly believes, that moment from Jesus a pardon receives." (Words by Fanny J. Crosby, 1875)*

There is nothing more burdensome, nothing heavier than guilt. It wears us out physically and emotionally, as well as spiritually. We all experience guilt because we all fall short in our attempts toward Christlikeness. The shorthand expression of all that is "sin." It's a word we may choose not to use, but that refusal doesn't make the truth of the word go away, and it does not lift the weight of guilt off our shoulders and heart. We need rest.

Rest is to be found in Jesus. We sing about it all the time. We rehearse the truth and availability of this rest on Wednesday or Thursday night. We celebrate the truth and availability of this rest on Sunday morning. And still, we often refuse to accept the truth. We need rest, but we won't let go of the heavy load.

You may recall the scientific film documentary several years ago (pre–*Animal Planet*) depicting monkeys being captured without any harmful traps or snares. A large piece of fruit was placed in a container with a small opening. The monkey would reach through the opening and grab hold of the fruit. The problem was that the fruit could not be pulled through the opening. The monkey was trapped, or so it thought. It was trapped only because it would not let go.

Pardon from our prison is as simple as letting go. "The vilest offender," Fanny Crosby reminds us, "who truly believes, that moment from Jesus a pardon receives." Letting go of our guilt lifts burdens and destroys traps. Watch for this news to appear in your choir folder. Believe it when you read it and share it as you sing it. It is good news. It is the gospel. It is rest.

Prayer: God, thank you for the gift of forgiveness. Help us to believe it, accept it for ourselves, and sing its good news to the congregation. In Jesus' name. Amen.

Hymn: *"On Jordan's Stormy Banks I Stand," stanza 4: "When [for] I shall see my Father's face, and in his bosom rest." (Words by Samuel Stennett, 1787)*

We sing toward heaven. We need to say that out loud and remind ourselves of it often. We sing toward heaven. The story in which we participate, the story that begins in Genesis and begins again forever in Revelation is a story that moves toward heaven. We are bound for the promised land.

The bracketed "for" is included in the verse above because that word is used in some hymnals, while "when" is used in others. Both tell the story. We sing "for" with full faith and confidence in God. We sing "when" as a longing for the day to come, or, perhaps better stated, rejoicing in the assurance that the day will come. Either way, we look forward to the day on which we "shall see [our] Father's face, and in his bosom rest."

The very thought brings songs from the depths of our heart whether we are singers or not. But you are a singer. Your song of heaven comes out on pitch and in harmony with the others in choir. Your song of heaven comes out in rhythm and with thoughtful dynamics. Those characteristics come with a responsibility. Your song of heaven can be a song of leadership, a song that says, "This way to the goal." Your song can rally the congregation and remind them of the hope of heaven. Your song can encourage them. Help the congregation to sing "when" and "for" with their hearts engaged and their eyes fixed on heaven.

Choir members are ministers assigned to a specific congregation. You have been assigned, not by a bishop, but by a King, the King of heaven. You are an ambassador, an angel, that is to say, a messenger. Your message: "I am bound for the promised land, I am bound for the promised land; oh, who will come and go with me? I am bound for the promised land." It is a land of rest. See it, sing it, know it.

Prayer: Dear God, thank you for the gift of heaven, even now. Thank you for how that gift enriches life with hope and peace. Fill our songs with your heaven. In Jesus' name. Amen.

Summer
Week 6

Scripture: "And God sent an angel to Jerusalem to destroy it; but when he was about to destroy it, the Lord took note and relented concerning the calamity; he said to the destroying angel, 'Enough! Stay your hand.' " (1 Chron. 21:15)

Here's a command to rest that is worth observing. King David had angered God. He did so by demanding that Joab and the commanders of David's army go out and count the troops. David wanted to know how powerful he was. Joab warned David that that was not a good idea. But David's crown outranked Joab's star so the general started to count. He got to 1.1 million and just didn't have the heart to keep counting. So he reported that number to David. Evidently, he knew that the number was big enough to impress David. But God was displeased and David realized it (vv. 7-8).

Gad, David's "seer," was God's messenger. He presented to David a not-so-tasty menu of punishments. David was allowed to choose. He chose the "three days of the sword of the Lord," which came with "pestilence on the land, and the angel of the LORD destroying throughout all the territory of Israel" (v. 12).

Seventy thousand people fell at the sword of God's angel (v. 14). The angel was moving toward 1.1 million when God said "Enough! Stay your hand." In other words, "Angel, take a rest."

David chose "three days of the sword of the LORD" because it was his only hope for mercy. The other two choices relied on "man" (specifically the enemies he'd been fighting) and "nature." If there was to be any hope for mercy, it would only be in God. David's faith in God averted greater disaster.

Mercy is a great place to rest. We rest there and God rests there. Indeed, we rest there together—you, me, all other Christians, and God. God's wrath takes a seat and we all rest. We should choose mercy in all our dealings with one another and with God. Sing the songs of mercy. Sing them with loving hearts.

Prayer: Lord Jesus Christ, Son of God, have mercy on me a sinner. Amen.

Hymn: *"Immortal, Invisible, God Only Wise," stanza 2: "Unresting, unhasting, and silent as light, nor wanting nor wasting, thou rulest in might." (Words by Walter Chalmers Smith, 1867)*

God, who rested on the seventh day of creation, never sleeps or slumbers. While God is unresting, when God the Creator came to earth as God the Son, this power was put aside. While on earth, Jesus needed rest like any other human. Now that Jesus has ascended and the presence of God is fully spiritual, we can look at God through Walter Chalmers Smith's eyes. His hymn is rooted in scripture.

Though God never sleeps, God is not in a hurry, doesn't make a lot of noise about work, and isn't wasteful. Yet, God rules in might. These attributes point to rest for us. How much extra energy do we use when we hurry to, through, and away from a task? How much noise do we make in our complaining, to whoever will listen, about our overcrowded schedules and workloads? How much do we waste in the consumption of fast, disposable, over-priced products? God calls us to rest. Slow to the pace of meaningful conversation, care for the environment (of which we are divinely appointed stewards), healthy eating, and proper rest. Friends, family, the earth, our bodies—these are gifts, but gifts with stewardship responsibilities built in.

Having said all that, however, the greatest rest implied in this hymn is found in the phrase "and silent as light." Think about the noise related to busy schedules and the work necessary to maintain our lifestyles. Our noisy efforts often produce a great deal of heat, but little light. Light is silent. Light is the environment of wisdom. Silence is the prelude and the postlude of things profound. Noise distracts and wastes. Hurry damages, destroys, and wastes.

The immortal, invisible, God only wise calls us to rest and to a restful pace. God calls us to rest from consuming ambition and waste. There is a song here, a quieting song for our hearts and our congregations.

Prayer: Dear God, slow us down. Make us aware of your creation and all good things around us. Forgive our hurry and our wastefulness, we pray. In Jesus' name. Amen.

Summer
Week 8

Hymn: "Shall We Gather at the River," stanza 4: "Soon we'll reach the shining river, soon our pilgrimage will cease; soon our happy hearts will quiver with the melody of peace." (Words by Robert Lowry, 1864)

Rest is not always possible at the exact time and place we want it. Sometimes we have to keep on keeping on. Even in those circumstances, however, rest is present. We know how long it has been since we have rested, we know how much we need it, and we know that eventually we will get it. Rest is a companion on the journey.

Rest may reside with the goal, but the reality of it is present and powerful. We press on singing with the others who are still on the path. "Soon we'll reach the shining river, soon our pilgrimage will cease; soon our happy hearts will quiver with the melody of peace." Wait a minute—"happy hearts"? We can almost hear the trudging of worn-out boots on the rocky path. We can almost feel the slope of the mountain the pilgrims are leaning into. We can almost press against the silence as we listen for the first faint sounds of the shining river. But Robert Lowry depicts these travelers as having happy hearts. Does that make sense?

Rest helps define work. Rest helps us understand that it's all about the journey. Work that is noble, contributing, and worth the effort, delights the soul. The journey that moves forward and upward enriches the soul. These are happy hearts. The Holy Spirit provides guidance and strength for the journey. My most important accomplishments are things that I don't want to do again. I can come to that conclusion with a wonderful sense of fulfillment when I sit down to rest and look back. The work and the journey are pleasing; they make my heart happy. I've had enough of those journeys to get up from my rest and start on the next journey with joy and confidence.

Are you at the beginning of a journey in your life, your choir, your congregation? Sing the melody of peace, now. Sing it as inspiration for yourself and others.

Prayer: Dear God, help us to face the challenge and begin the journey singing, from the very beginning, the melody of peace, the song of the rest that awaits. In Jesus' name. Amen.

Scripture: *"Then the mariners were afraid, and each cried to his god. They threw the cargo that was in the ship into the sea, to lighten it for them. Jonah, meanwhile, had gone down into the hold of the ship and had lain down, and was fast asleep." (Jon. 1:5)*

Jonah wasn't resting, he was hiding. He didn't like the work God had called him to, so he ran and hid. Sleep was his deepest hiding place. In fact, it wasn't the work that he disliked so much. It was the potential outcome that sent him running the other way. He didn't want the people of Nineveh to repent and enjoy the blessings of God. He had good, though hard, news to share. He didn't mind beating the people of Nineveh over the head with the message, but he was not excited about the prospects of them paying attention and moving from being candidates for God's wrath to becoming candidates for God's love. He didn't mind singing, but not this song to these people.

That seems unimaginable. Why would someone have important, even good, news and be hesitant to share it with the people who most need it?

Is there anyone in the congregation (or in your choir) who is "on your last nerve"? How do you feel about serving them by lovingly leading them into worship? Would you rather run to your den and take a nap? In a strange way, such reactions are deep statements of faith in God and God's good news. We believe it will work. It's just that sometimes, we're not sure we want it to work.

There is a sea of frightened "mariners" out there in the pews on Sunday morning. Some are attending out of the logic of the old saying "any port in a storm." Others are aboard "the old ship of Zion" simply because they are bone tired of swimming with the sharks. The mariners in the storm-tossed ship were not ready to perish: "The captain came and said to [Jonah], 'What are you doing sound asleep? Get up, call on your god! Perhaps the god will spare us a thought so that we do not perish.'" The captain speaks for the congregation.

Wake from your sleep that is not rest and sing. Sing the hard songs. Sing the good news songs. Sing the songs that just might work.

Prayer: Dear God, wake us up to the power of your good news and to our responsibility to sing it out, even to those who are drowning in our disdain. In Jesus' name. Amen.

Summer
Week 10

Hymn: "He Leadeth Me: O Blessed Thought," stanza 4: "And when my task on earth is done, when by thy grace the victory's won, even death's cold wave I will not flee, since God through Jordan leadeth me." (Words by Joseph H. Gilmore, 1862)

Even Christians prefer the euphemism "final rest" rather than "death." But death is the word and death is the event. The good news is that we don't have to cross Jordan alone.

At age 45 I underwent heart surgery to have my aortal valve replaced. There were complications during the procedure. I am told they nearly "lost" me (another euphemism). I don't know if what I am about to tell you occurred while I was "out" or if it is a poetic processing of all that I now know happened to me in the operating room. Whatever its place in the sequence of events, the scene was and is real to me.

Jesus and I stood on the bank of a river. It didn't appear to be wide like the Mississippi in New Orleans, and I did not have the impression it was that deep. It was however, a river to be reckoned with if one wanted to get to the other side. I was not alone on its banks. Jesus stood with me. His presence was like that of a good friend. He was calm and confident. He asked if I wanted to cross over. Aware of who he was I said, "It seems to me that's pretty much up to you." He said, "Come along then, let's walk a little further along the bank. We can cross over at any time."

I am not afraid of death. I can call it that—death. Some day, Jesus and I will step in and wade across. For the time being, there are tasks to be done and victories for Jesus to win while I tag along. Someday we'll cross the river.

Is the song beginning to sound in your heart? Is your soul humming? Mine does frequently. The song is this fourth stanza: "And when my task on earth is done, when by thy grace the victory's won, even death's cold wave I will not flee, since God through Jordan leadeth me." I rest in that stanza of that hymn. The cold wave will be no problem when you are holding God's warm hand.

Prayer: Dear God, thank you for sending Jesus to wade across the river with us. Help us to walk with him along the bank as well. It is in his name we pray. Amen.

Hymn: "Break Thou the Bread of Life," stanza 2: "Bless thou the truth, dear Lord, to me, to me, as thou didst bless the bread by Galilee; then shall all bondage cease, all fetters fall; and I shall find my peace, my all in all." (Words by Mary A. Lathbury, 1877)

The truth shall set you free. God's word was inspired at the time of writing and is inspiring when we read it. The Holy Spirit interprets, blesses, and helps us apply the truth of the Bible. The hymns and anthems we sing are direct quotes of, or are based on, the Bible. Somehow we know the difference when something non-scriptural is sung in worship. Something doesn't ring true when we bring anything other than scripture or scriptural truth into the sanctuary on Sunday morning.

We need to revisit truth that is higher than our opinion and deeper than our desires. We need to revisit truth that is wiser than our prejudice and richer than our knowledge. We need to revisit truth that shapes us and gives us a break from our attempts to shape facts for our benefit. We all have access to the Bible, but few take advantage of that availability.

Enter the choir. You break the bread of life every Sunday. Every Sunday! It is broken for you by your choir director at every rehearsal as you are preparing for ministry and worship leadership. Then you process into the choir loft, as ministers, and you break and distribute the bread. Our prayer then becomes, "Bless thou the truth, dear Lord, to me, to me, as thou didst bless the bread by Galilee." We revise the prayer toward God's further intent by asking the Lord to bless the truth "for them, for them" as we sing.

When the Bible is being opened, read, sung, and received in the context of worship, bondage ceases, fetters fall, and peace is found. Sing and rest in the truth of it.

Prayer: Dear God, give us a new hunger for your word and then bless the reading, teaching, preaching, and singing of it for our growth and your glory. In Jesus' name. Amen.

Summer
Week 12

Scripture: "When Jesus came to the place, he looked up and said to him, 'Zacchaeus, hurry and come down; for I must stay at your house today.' "
(Luke 19:5)

Choir members need to come down now and then to provide a place for Jesus to rest. There are two trees that choir members often rest in. One is the tree of talent. We get up this tree if we think the choir cannot function without us or that it is musically below us. Jesus calls us to come down out of that tree so that we might humbly participate in the community and give him a place to stay.

Another tree that choir members often climb to watch the parade go by is the choir loft itself. We get up there and decide that we can see all we need to see and stay above the crush of the crowd. It's a perch where we appear to be involved and interested, but it can be a great hiding place. Jesus calls us to come down and be a part of the larger and broader life and work of the congregation. He is out among the people and he wants us to come join him so he can stay at our house today. He calls us to ministry now. That is where he is going to be, and he wants us to provide a place for him—the place where we live. He wants to come and stay in our comfortable spot, but we must come down to meet him.

The choir can be a wonderful community, but it is not the entire congregation. For the choir to lead the congregation in worship, the choir must come from the crowd. Choir members must join the parade. Some of us will have to "come down" to do that. Jesus shouldn't have to look up to find us. We should be at his side. Among the crowd, ministering.

Zacchaeus came down and it didn't take long for him to see his life as Jesus saw it. He gained a new and humble perspective. He started giving back to the community what they had been giving him, with interest. Choir member, come down, so that you can sing from the heart of the community.

Prayer: Dear God, forgive us for the times we think we are above it all, times when we think we are better than the crowd. Lord, help me down out of the tree and welcome you to my house today. In Jesus' name. Amen.

Even though singers work to keep them "alive," the half notes on the "Melt me, mold me," phrase are places to rest. We have time to think about the Holy Spirit's work of "melting." Then we have time to think about the word "me." Then we have time to think about the Holy Spirit's work of "molding." That is followed by another focus on "me." We are only halfway there. Now we have time, two beats, to think about the Holy Spirit's work of "filling." Then, you guessed it, time to focus on "me." Finally, we have time to think about the Holy Spirit's work of "using." It is followed, of course, by time to ponder what it means for "me" to be used by the Holy Spirit.

By the end of that line in the song, tongues of fire are on our heads and in our hearts. We are hearing the interpretations of melt, mold, fill, and use in our own language, the language of our thoughts and prayers and life. Everyone is hearing God's message in their own language.

The Holy Spirit is resting on us and we have a song to sing. It is a song of the power of God the Spirit. It is a song of hearts warmed to flame and tongues sharpened by the truth. Sing the song in the Spirit. Sing the song in awe. Sing the song in humility, yet with boldness.

The Holy Spirit has enlivened the Church. Make sure it shows up in the music of the choir and congregation. Rest in the fact that the Holy Spirit is providing the vision and energy and is fully capable of managing the results. Sing the words of this song, assured that the Holy Spirit will interpret the moanings behind them.

Prayer: Dear God, thank you for the presence of the Holy Spirit. Thank you for vision, guidance, comfort, and encouragement. Help us to rest in these. In Jesus' name. Amen.

Index of Hymns

Index of Scripture